FOLLOW ME

DISCIPLESHIP

YVETTE M. MURPHY

ISBN 978-1-957582-87-0 (paperback)
ISBN 978-1-957582-86-3 (digital)

Printed in the United States of America

Contents

Preface

People of God, it's time to shift (move quickly) into **"Radical Discipleship"** mode. Jesus commanded saying, Go therefore making disciples of all nations. (see Matthew 28:19) It's time to change your posture and do the work of the Kingdom of God. The Word of God is the power tool used to draw people or return other's back to the One and Only Living God. For He is the Father of our Lord and Savior Jesus Christ. So, let us go and cause a domino affect in the earth as the disciples did in times past.

Let's pray this prayer together

God of the harvest, I come to you with a thankful heart and an attitude of gratitude. You are the Greatest of all times who has called, empowered and equipped me to be a fisher of men, women, boys and girls. You have clothed me in boldness. You taught me to stand flat footed against any opposition. I am going forward in my assignment with an opened mouth speaking the Word of truth. I ask that you would remove every distraction from the peoples minds so that Your word will be the knock at the door of their hearts. Let their mind be the storage container that stores Your word. I pray that they would open their mouths and declare Your Word when life's issues try to knock them down. In Jesus name. Amen.

Now that you have made your request, be attentive and obedient when the Lord speaks to you. There are no more excuses for you to do nothing nor for you to stay behind the walls of the church and witness to church members. There are others who don't attend church who needs to hear what God has to say to them. Go and serve heavens menu. The appetizer is to have faith in God. The main course is to love God with all your heart and to love your enemies as yourself. The dessert is to believe in Jesus Christ.

It's time to go fishing!

Throw out your net and reach those who don't attend church. Show compassion with those who have been hurt by people in the church. Encourage him or her who say church people are phony. Let them know that they're not attending church service for the people but they are in service to hear and put in practice the Word of God for themselves. Advise them to begin building a relationship with God through Christ Jesus. In (**John 14:6 NLT**) Jesus says, I am the way, the truth and the life: no one can come to the Father except through me.

NEWS FLASH

Whatever you do, do not discriminate: Jesus said, Go therefore and make disciples of all nations [helping the people to learn of Me, believe in Me, and obey My words], baptizing them in the name of the Father and of the Son and of the Holy Spirit, teaching them to observe everything that I have commanded you; and lo, I am with you always [remaining with you perpetually-- regardless of circumstances, and on every occasion], even to the end of the age. (**Matthew 28:19-20 AMP**)

Introduction

What is a disciple/discipleship? Disciple is defined as someone who follows; or a learner. The standard definition of disciple is someone who adheres to the teachings of another. Disciple/Discipleship are defined as One who embraces and assists in spreading the teaching of another.

Disciple refers to someone who takes up the ways of someone else, who learns from him to live like him. Jesus is the One believers should want to follow and have a relationship with, building their lives reflecting His light to all people.

Disciple/Discipleship is an open invitation and it does not matter who you are, where you come from, who you are related to or your educational background, etc.

What does it mean to be a disciple of Jesus Christ?

In (**John 13:34-35 NKJV**) Jesus said, A new commandment I give to you, That you love one another; as I have loved you, that you also love one another. By this all men will know that you are My disciples, if you have love for one another. We should always dress ourselves in love, displaying and utilizing (put to use, apply) Christlike characteristics in our everyday life. Even if you're not having a good day, do not destroy your representation of Christ. Do your best, even if you have to excuse yourself because your flesh is trying to be in control and the devil wants you to fell.

In this discipleship book, you will find that we are called to be disciples of Jesus Christ in whom we believe and have faith in. In the Gospel According to Matthew, Mark and Luke, you'll find their individual accounts of Jesus' requirements to follow Him. You will find some differences but they all came to the realization that following Him requires a few adjustments in a person's life.

When you put your mind to living for Christ, life will become much more loving, peaceful and enjoyable. Keep in mind that change is a process and everything is not going to become new overnight. It takes patience and let patience have her perfect work. (see James 1:4) So when you begin working on the new you, life will still have its ups and downs, laughs and cries. There will be days when you become uncomfortable and unease but stand firm on God's promises for your life. (see Philippians 1:6) Stay encouraged, trust, depend, and have confidence in Him. Don't rush the process, it is making you a better you.

Jesus' first four Disciples

As Jesus was walking by the Sea of Galilee, He saw Simon called Peter and his brother Andrew. They were throwing out their nets into the sea for they were fishermen. He looked at them and said Follow Me; I'll make you fishers of men and women. I'll show you how to catch them. At that moment they dropped their nets, and followed Him. Moving forward from there, Jesus noticed two other brothers James the son of Zebedee, and his brother John. They were sitting in a boat with Zebedee their father preparing their nets to go fishing and Jesus called them. He told them they would be fishers of people as well. Without delay they abandoned the boat and their father and followed Him. [Matthew 4:18-22]

Individual Writings

Matthew 16:24-27 (NKJV)
Then Jesus said to His disciples, "If anyone desires to come after Me, let him deny himself, and take up his cross, and follow Me. For whoever desires to save his life will lose it, but whoever loses his life for My sake

will find it. For what profit is it to a man if he gains the whole world, and loses his own soul? Or what will a man give in exchange for his soul? For the Son of Man will come in the glory of His Father with His angels, and then He will reward each according to his works.

In Mark 8:34-38 [NKJV] you will find Jesus' specific requirements for being His disciple: When He had called the people to Himself, with His disciples also, He said to them, Whoever desires to come after Me, let him deny himself, and take up his cross, and follow Me. For whoever desires to save his life will lose it, but whoever loses his life for My sake and the gospel's will save it. For what will it profit a man if he gains the whole world, and loses his own soul? Or what will a man give in exchange for his soul? For whoever is ashamed of Me and My words in this adulterous and sinful generation, of him the Son of Man also will be ashamed when He comes in the glory of His Father with the holy angels.

Luke 9:23-26 (KJV)
And he said to them all, If any man will come after me, let him deny himself, and take up his cross daily and follow me. For whosoever will save his life shall lose it: but whosoever will lose his life for my sake, the same shall save it. For what is a man advantaged, if he gain the whole world, and lose himself, or be cast away? For whosoever shall be ashamed of me and of my words, of him shall the Son of man be ashamed, when he shall come in his own glory, and in his Father's and of the holy angels.

What is Required on the Journey of Discipleship

Listed below you will find what Jesus said we **must do** to follow Him.

Whoever desires - Jesus is speaking to the crowd, the call and choice is for whoever desires. Jesus is not forcing you to follow Him. It is totally up to you. Desire in Greek is (thělō, *thel'o*) meaning to will. Jesus sent out the invitation and "the choice is yours." You don't need to make any excuses, it's either yes or no. In [**Matthew 8:21 NLT**] Another one of his disciples said, "Lord, first let me return home and bury my father." But Jesus told him, "Follow me now. Let the spiritually dead bury their own dead." In [**Luke 9:61-62 NLT**] Another said, "Yes, Lord, I will follow you, but first let me say good-bye to my family." But Jesus told him, "Anyone who puts a hand to the plow and then looks back is not fit for the Kingdom of God." **So, let's not turn desire into disaster.**

Deny himself - meaning to reject, restrain, refuse and remove "self" completely out of the way. The word deny makes people uncomfortable because they want to do whatever they want to, when they want to, how they want it to be done and where they want to go without being questioned. And if anyone don't know, here is an eye opener, **we are in a selfish, "me, myself and I" world**. But Christ wants us to take the attention off ourselves, caring only about oneself and ones own needs. He does not want us to ignore or overlook helping someone else. So, if you are **able and available** to feed someone when they are hungry share your food or if someone needs a ride to work give them a ride and keep it moving. If you're not able, maybe you know someone who can help them out and when you do that, keep it to yourself because your Father who sees in secret will Himself reward you openly. [**Refer to Matthew 6:1-4**] Jesus came to show us how to live unselfishly and not to think only of ourselves. We should want to do better if we want to be like Jesus Christ. He is full of compassion.

Listed below you will find a few scriptures from the Old and the New Testament of the Lord's compassion:

Psalm 86:15 (NKJV) But You, O Lord, are a God full of compassion, and gracious, Longsuffering and abundant in mercy and truth.

Lamentations 3:22-23 (KJV) It is of the Lord's mercies that we are not consumed, because his compassions fail not. They are new every morning: Great is thy faithfulness.

Matthew 14:14 (NLT] Jesus saw the huge crowd as he stepped from the boat, and he had compassion on them and healed their sick.

I Peter 3:8 [AMP] Finally, all of you be like-minded [united in spirit], sympathetic, brotherly, kind-hearted [courteous and compassionate toward each other as members of one household,] and humble in spirit.

Take up your cross

Speaks of enduring hardship, persecution and trials because of your belief in Jesus Christ. In [**Matthew 5:11-12 NLT**] "God blesses you when people mock you and persecute you and lie about you and say all sorts of evil things against you because you are my followers. Be happy about it! Be very glad! For a great reward awaits you in heaven. And remember, the ancient prophets were persecuted in the same way.

Everyone has their own cross to carry and you're not alone because Jesus said in [**Matthew 28:20 NLT**] And be sure of this; I am with you always, even to the end of the age.

This is a public announcement that you've enrolled as a soldier in the "Armies of God." Be strong in the Lord and in the power of His might, depending and relying on Him to bring you through. Keep in mind that you are not wrestling against flesh and blood but against evil ruler's and authorities in the unseen world. We must put on the whole armor of God everyday so that we're fully equipped and protected from the enemy and every scheme he has arranged to overthrow or defeat us. [See to Eph. 6:1-18].

Take Heart! Jesus defeated His adversaries and overcame a life of hard knocks from the religious leaders. He plowed through all of the nonsense and you can plow through yours as well. You have the power to demolish every negative opponent by speaking the word of God in any situation that comes to frustrate you or take your peace.

The journey is tight but it's right with God being the Head General of the **"Just and Righteous Militia."** He is **Jehovah Magen** "The Lord my Shield" He will protect you. He is **El-Roi** "The God who sees." He sees everything. He gives us encouragement in times of trouble. In [Psalm 46:1] God is our refuge and strength, A very present help in trouble.

In spite of what's going on you can make it with God on you side. Don't forfeit your blessings. The Lord of Hosts is holding you in His hands.

In **Matthew 5:10-12 (NCV)** Blessed are those who are persecuted for doing good, for the kingdom of heaven belongs to them. "People will insult you and hurt you. They will lie and say all kinds of evil things about you because you follow me. But when they do, you will be blessed. Rejoice and be glad, because you have a great reward waiting for you in heaven. People did the same evil things to the prophets who lived before you.

Stay on your guard and remain steadfast. Keep your head up and don't allow yourself to become agitated due to negative words that you hear. Remember, you were told beforehand what will happen to you because you are a follower of Jesus Christ. So, don't stop doing the work of the

Lord. Continue going forward carrying your cross and being not ashamed of the Gospel of Jesus Christ our Lord. The prophets who were before you were persecuted but they continued their work and you should do as they have done. Run the race that is set before you.

Follow Me - Follow in Hebrew is (hâlak, *haw-lak'*) which means to walk, live in a certain way, go forward. Your past **"Without Jesus"** have become a lifestyle of *"I'm Yours Forever."* Now that you have agreed to follow Jesus, your atmosphere should display the "The Fruit of the Spirit." [see Galatians 5:22-23] So, live a life that displays the Light of Christ and imitate Him. [refer to Ephesians 5:1-2 NLT] Walk in His ways and He will direct your steps. He will lead you in the right direction with total access to operate in His amazing power. He will also download in your spirit the plans He have for you that will impact the lives of His people local and/or global.

In [Mark 2:13-17] Jesus was out by the lake again. A large crowd followed Him and He taught them. Jesus saw Levi, who is also called Matthew [Matthew 9:9-13, 10:3; Luke 5:27-32] working at the tax office. He said to Levi Follow Me and without hesitation Levi got up and followed Him. Later that day, Jesus along with His disciples and many sinners were having dinner at Levi's house. When the teachers of the Law of Moses saw the crowd that Jesus was eating with they sarcastically said to His disciples Oh! Now He's hanging out with these sinners and greedy tax collectors! When Jesus over heard them, He said people who are healthy don't need a physician but people who are sick do. I didn't come to invite good people to be My followers but to invite sinners.

Keep holding on and let Jesus led you through this journey of ups and downs, mountaintop and valley experiences. No matter which of these you go through, you will make it with Jesus on your side.

Following Jesus will cost you something - The cost of being a disciple has nothing to do with money and it is said best in [Matthew 16:24.] Then Jesus said to his disciples, If anyone desires to be My disciple, let him deny himself [disregard, lose sight of, and forget himself and his own interests] and take up his cross and follow Me [cleave steadfastly to Me, conform wholly to My example in living and, if need be, in dying also].

As you think on the cost and what it takes to follow Christ, you **MUST** believe and have faith that He has already completed everything you need. Do you believe? If so, don't allow yourself to become overwhelmed or angry about what you're giving up? It's only a test of your faith. Ask the Lord what do He want you to give up. Trust and believe that the Lord **WILL** provide. He did it for Abram/Abraham. In [Gen. 12:1-3] Abram obeyed God when he was told to leave his country, and his father's family and go to the land that God will show him. God made him a great nation, and blessed him exceedingly, abundantly.

In [Gen. 22:1-9] God tested Abraham's faith. Abraham was told to offer his only son Isaac, whom he loves as a burnt offering. So, Abraham built an altar and tied Isaac to it. Then he picked up a knife to slay Isaac but the angel of the Lord provided a ram in a bush instead of his son.

Never count God out. He will replace what you gave up.

<u>God in Three Persons</u> - God the Father, God the Son, God the Holy Spirit.

Genesis 1:1-2 (AMP) In the beginning God (prepared, formed, fashioned, and) created the heavens and the earth. The earth was without form, and an empty waste, and darkness was upon the face of the very deep. The Spirit of God was moving (hovering, brooding) over the face of the waters. Everything began with God speaking and by the word of His mouth the heavens and earth were established. The earth had no form... describing chaos before God put all things in order.

In the beginning: God who is the Creator of the heavens and the earth! He is omniscience (all knowing) and the first of any and everyone. He knew exactly how much light the earth needed before He positioned the sun, the moon and the stars. He knew the amount of weight the clouds would need to keep its position; He measured the distance and the time each of them needed to operate.

The earth: was out of shape and darkness covered the oceans. It had a lack of activities, human's and purpose. God had a plan even though nothing had existed at the time. He knew what He was about to create and He displayed His splendor upon creation.

The Spirit of God: was moving over the waters and He was in protection mode like our Shepherd (Jesus Christ) protects us (His sheep). In **John 10:28-30** Jesus says no one is able to snatch us away from Him, for the Father gave us to Him and He is more powerful than anyone else. No one can snatch us from the Father's hand. The Father and I are one. Jesus has given us encouraging words that we are safe and secure in them.

Then God the Father spoke the three words that brought forth His glorious creation, "Let there be." God's splendor is displayed everywhere and it is visible at all times.

Genesis 1:26 [AMP] God said, Let Us make mankind in Our image, after Our likeness, and let them have complete authority over the fish of the sea, the birds of the air, the (tame) beasts, and over all of the earth, and over everything that creeps upon the earth.

1. **Let Us** speaks of the three persons of the God Head, Holy Trinity (God the Father, God the Son, God the Holy Spirit).
2. **Make mankind in Our image:** We (humans) were made to be God's reflection on the earth, and to be **ruler's** over everything He made [refer to Psalm 8:1-9 NCV]..
3. **After Our likeness:** God made human beings to be just like them. He gave us intellectual abilities, moral and certain ethical responsibilities. God had given Adam ruler-ship over everything. He was given dominion over the fish in the sea, the birds of the air and every living thing that moves on the earth. What he once ruled had become his loss because of his disobedience.

John 1:1 (KJV) In the beginning was the Word, and the Word was with God, and the Word was God. **John 1:14 (KJV)** And the Word was made flesh, and dwelt among us, (and we beheld his glory, the glory as of the only begotten of the Father,) full of grace and truth. Word in Greek is logos

1. **In the beginning** God and Jesus has always been in existence. [Refer to: John 8:58]
2. **The Word was with God** implying an intimate relationship (Father and Son). They have equal status. John 10:30 [NKJV] I and My Father are one.
3. **The Word was God** gives emphasis to oneness and unity Hebrews 1:1-4 [AMP]. The Word became human [Jesus Christ] John 1:14

Jesus performs miracles

Jesus' arrival was much needed. He demonstrated His power and authority among the people. Listed below are a few of His miracles.

1. Jesus healed multitudes who were sick, deaf, mute and those who had diseases. [Matthew 14:34-36; 15:29-32]; [Mark 6:53-57, 7:31-37]
2. He fed the multitude(s). [Matthew 14:13-21; 15:32-39]; [Mark 6:30-44, 8:1-10]; [Luke 9:10-17]; [John 6:1-14]
3. Lazarus returns to life [John 11:38-44]
   Jairus daughter was reintroduced to her family and a woman having a blood extravasation was healed [Matthew 9:18-26]; [Mark 5:21--43]; [Luke 8:40-56]; [Mark 5:25-34]
4. Jesus power over two men who were controlled by demons [Matthew 8:28-34]; [Mark 5:1-20]; [Luke 8:26-39]

Jesus' Power over Sin

Jesus's death brought us justice and now we are morally righteous. He has the power to forgive us of our sin. I John 1:9 (NKJV) says, If we confess our sins, He is faithful and just to forgive us our sins and to cleanse us from all unrighteousness. In the Old Testament, God spoke to Moses saying speak to the children of Israel saying "If a person sins...**Refer to: Leviticus 4: 1-4, [AMPC]**. In the New Testament, John one of Jesus' Apostles recorded in [**I John 2:2 AMPC**] He [that same Jesus Himself] is the propitiation (the atoning sacrifice) for our sins and not only our sins but also for [the sins of] the whole world.

Jesus stepped in on our behalf and finalized the sin debt for the entire world which pleased God. This was done once and for all. Jesus' last words on the cross were "It is finished!" And bowing His head, He gave up His spirit. [**Refer to: John 19:30**]

Dwelt Among us-the Hebrew word for dwelt is [**chânâh khaw-naw**] meaning to camp, dwell, to encamp, grow to an end, lie, pitch (tent), rest in tent.

Among in Hebrew is (ʿîm, **eem**) meaning accompanying, against, and (× long as), before, beside, by (reason of), for all, from (among, between), in, like, more than, of, (un-) to, with (-al).

- God said to Moses, tell the children of Israel to make Him a sanctuary (holy place) so that His presence (glory) would dwell with them. **Refer to: Exodus 25:8 [KJV]**
  The glory of God (shekinah glory) appeared in a thick cloud filling the Temple of God, and the priest could not stand to minister. *Refer to: I Kings 8:11 [NJKV]*
- Jesus lived among the people and they saw His glory. Jesus took three of the disciples (Peter, James and John) on a high mountain and He had a metamorphose (to change in wholly appearance) before them. *Refer to: Matthew 17:1-4 [NKJV]*; [**Mark 9:2-4**]

Holy Spirit is our Comforter John 14:16 (AMPC) says, And I will ask the Father, and He will give you another Comforter (Counselor, Helper, Intercessor, Advocate, Strengthener, and Standby), that He may remain with you forever. Jesus had requested that the Father send us the Holy Spirit (the Comforter). Jesus knew that we would need help because there will be trouble (spiritually, emotionally, physically and financially) in our lives that we could not handle by ourselves.

Holy Spirit is the Spirit of Truth John 14:26 [KJV] says But the Comforter, which is the Holy Ghost whom the Father will send in my name. He shall teach you all things, and bring all things to your remembrance, whatsoever I have said unto you.

In this passage of scripture Jesus gives the disciples words of encouragement and assuring them that help is on the way. We as disciples in the twenty first century have received these same words of encouragement as well. Holy Spirit takes residence in the heart of all believers. Let us who believe in Jesus change the world upside down just as the disciples did in past times. We are fishers of men for the Kingdom of God and there is no time to lose heart. There is unlimited power living on the inside of us and it's ready to be activated. There is no more excuses because the Spirit of Truth will lead and guide us. He is our GPS and know exactly the direction we are to take.

Jesus I am names

The Gospel According to John was written by John who called himself "the disciple whom Jesus loved." This John is not John the Baptist. This John was the disciple who leaned on Jesus' bosom at the Last Supper. He reveals Jesus' deity and gives detailed information on His "I am" names. John was a disciple who became an apostle. [see Matthew 10:1] He is also the one standing by the cross at Jesus' crucifixion and He said to him "Behold your mother!" [John 19:27]

Now John the Baptist was one of Jesus' announcer's who said, I am The voice of one crying in the wilderness: Make straight the way of the LORD. [John 1:23b] Isaiah the prophet was the other announcer saying; The voice of one crying in the wilderness: Prepare the way of the LORD; Make straight in the desert A highway for our God. [Isaiah 40:3]

John the Baptist was calling for the people to repent and turn back God. He also baptized them in Bethabara beyond the Jordan. [John 1:28]

John the Baptist never crumbled under pressure, even when he was being questioned by the Pharisees. They asked "Why are you baptizing if you are not the Christ, nor Elijah, nor the Prophet. John answered saying, I baptize with water, but... [See John 1:24-28 NKJV]

The next day John saw Jesus coming toward him and said, "Behold! The Lamb of God who takes away the sin of the world!" This is He of whom I said, After me comes a Man who is preferred before me, for He was before me... [See John 1:29-31 NKJV]

"I am" tells us that our everyday physical and spiritual necessities are truly linked together in Jesus Christ. For in Him we live, and move, and have our being. (Acts 17:28)

I am the Bread of Life (John 6:35, 41, 48 & 58)

"Bread of life" means, bread that provides life. Jesus is the Only One who is able to fulfill our hunger and thirst. Jesus said to them, I am the bread of the life. He who comes to Me shall never hunger, and he who believes in Me shall never thirst. This is the bread of which came down from heaven not as your father's ate the manna, and are dead. He who eats this bread will live forever. Jesus wants to give you a life that is completely nourished, lacking nothing. He will supply all of your spiritual and physical needs. You must believe and take Him at His word. In [Psalm 119:89] Forever, O Lord, Your word is settled in heaven. His word does not change. You can always depend on Him who never changes. **Believing in Him will keep you from hunger and thirst.**

The Jewish council gave Jesus a hard time because He said He was the bread that came down from heaven. They were looking at a smaller picture. They asked, Is not this Jesus, the son of Joseph, whose father and mother we know? How is it then that He says, 'I have come down from heaven? [see John 6:41-42.] They were seeing Him through their natural lenses instead of looking through their spiritual eyes. We (believers) should not be like they were; it was one thing after another with them. Let's do better so that we can be better.

I am the light of the world – John 8:12
Jesus' identity has been revealed as the light of the world to all nations and people. He is the only true spiritual light. You must have a made-up mind to follow Him, and you will not walk in darkness. You will have the light that gives life to lead you.

Jesus is our light in darkness who uncovers and forgives sin. In [1 John 1:9] If we confess our sins, He is faithful and just to forgive us of our sins and to cleanse us from all unrighteous.

In John 8:3 [CEV] There was a woman that was caught in bed with a man that was not her husband. The scribes and Pharisees who followed the Law of Moses brought her to Jesus while He was teaching in the temple. These men were stuck on the Law which commanded them to throw big stones at her to kill her. They said to Jesus, what do you say? They asked Him this question to trap Him with His own words and accuse Him of breaking the Law of Moses. He knew what they were thinking. We should always remember that Jesus knows our every thought.

How quickly did the scribes and Pharisees forget they too had sinned? Jesus have His own way of doing things. He just started writing in the dirt. They kept annoying Him so He stood up and said "The one who never had a sinful desire, throw the first stone at her." He bent down again and wrote some more. After hearing that, they slowly left the crowd one at a time starting with the oldest ones until it was just Jesus and her. Jesus did not condemn her but He poured out His amazing grace over her. He told her to leave and don't sin anymore.

I am the door to the sheep – John 10:7,9 [A story told by Jesus to explain His religious message]
Jesus is the gate for believers. All who enters in through Him will be saved. But if they climb in by a different way, they are up to no good.

They can not be trusted. But you can always trust in Jesus. For He is the door and the Shepherd of His people. He knows you by name, He will lead, guide and protect you from dangers that you can and can not see. When you follow Him, He will give you an abundance of life that you would never have imagined. You will be a well fed, spiritually fat, increasing in wisdom and knowledge, expanding in understanding child of God. Just remember to stay on guard because there are wolves out there who wants to scatter the sheep. [refer to: John 10:10]

Be watchful for the false imitators because they will rob you spiritually. You must put them on notice that you are following Christ who leads you into all truth. Shout out aloud! I am unstoppable! Hallelujah!

I am the good shepherd – John 10:11-14 [A story told by Jesus to explain His religious message] Jesus is the good shepherd. The good shepherd came to give His life for His people. [refer to: John 3:16] He came to save the lost and give them eternal life. Jesus is our Love Physician and He takes care of us. The hired helper will not protect the sheep. He will abandon them because they do not belong to him. He is only in it for the money.

This is reality! There are some who say that they care for your soul but you are slowly being lead away from the truth. Open your heart and let Jesus in. He wants to live inside of you. Heart to Heart. He is love when you don't feel lovable. He is joy when you're sad. He is your peace when your atmosphere is in disorder. He is rest when you're restless. He is more than enough. Let Him be your dwelling place for eternity.

I am the resurrection and the life – John 11:25
Jesus is the resurrected Christ to all believers who are physically dead. He is life to those who believe and are presently alive. Jesus made it known that He have the power to restored life back into Lazarus. Jesus received a message from Martha and Mary saying Lazarus His beloved friend is sick. Jesus already knew that Lazarus' sickness will not end in death. Absolutely Not! God's glory will be revealed so that the Son of God may be glorified. Jesus and the disciples stayed where they were for two more days. He knew by delaying His return, the disciples and those who had

been comforting Martha and Mary would see up close and in the open His resurrection power.

He and the disciples talked about Lazarus being sick and that he will get well. Jesus finally said to them that Lazarus was died. He told the disciples that He was happy for them that He wasn't there; so that they may believe, trust and depend on Him. So, they headed out and after all that Jesus had said to them, Thomas continued in doubt. He told the other disciples let's go and die with Jesus. Jesus is about to show them what resurrected life looks like. And Thomas belief is about to become unshakable.

When Martha heard that Jesus wasn't far away, she ran out and met with Him. She was upset with Him saying, if You was here Lazarus wouldn't have died. And at this very moment, I know that whatever you ask God for He will give You. Jesus said to her Lazarus will rise. Why was Martha so quick to believe that God would answer Jesus' request? But slow to believe that Jesus will resurrect Lazarus right them. We can believe and be happy when other people say that God answered their prayer but doubt that God will answer your prayer.

Jesus said, I am the resurrection and I am the life; Whoever believes in Me will have life, even if they die, will live. And everyone who lives and believe in Me will never die. Do you believe? She replied, Yes Lord, I believe that You are the Messiah, God's Son who was coming into the world. She returned home and talked with Mary privately saying, Jesus wants to talk with you. Mary arrived blaming Jesus for the death of her brother as well. She said the same as Martha said to Him, if you... But it didn't matter to Him if He was there or not. He is still able "at this moment" to perform a resurrection miracle. He will use you to resurrect a dead situation. Do you believe? Jesus would soon turn their sadness into joy. Jesus prayed and God answered. Hallelujah! He called Lazarus to come forward and presented him alive. Jesus will also raise all who believe in Him at the last day. Is there anything you need to be resurrected in your life? If so, ask God in faith, in Jesus' name. Jesus is our Resurrection King now and forever! Glory to God in the Highest.

I am the way and the truth and the life – John 14:6
Jesus is the road that takes us to God. There is no other way to get to the Father but through Christ. He is the truth revealing God to us. He is the life, communicating between God and mankind. We need to stay in contact with Him at all times. He is our One an Only path to God. This is why our hearts and minds should be on "Jesus' mode." Let our relationship be a never- ending relationship with Him.

Jesus begins this chapter saying; Don't be unsettled in your heart. You're confident in God, put that same confidence in Me. My Father is running over with rooms in His house; if that wasn't true, I wouldn't have said anything to you. I'm going to get your room ready so it will be available for you when I come back and you will live with Me.

At this point, Thomas should have known the road. When you think someone knows you, think again. Just because a person has been around you for some time it doesn't mean that they really know you. Jesus said to Thomas, I am the road, also the truth, also the life. If you had really known Me, you would have known My Father also; and from now on you know Him and have seen Him. [John 14:7 NKJV]

Now Philip expresses his lack of seeing the Father. The Father has always been with them. Jesus is in God and God is in Jesus. They are one. [see John 10:30] There is no separation between them. It's Two in One. God the Father, God the Son. It's also One more of the God Head. God the Holy Spirit. Altogether it's Three in One. Trinity! Hallelujah!

I John 1:1-2
We want to tell you about the word that gives life, the One who existed before the world began. This is the One we have heard and have seen with our own eyes. We saw what He did and our own hands touched Him. Yes, the One whose life we saw up close. We are witnesses. We are now telling you about Him. He is the eternal life who has always existed with God the Father and was made visible to us.

In this 21ˢᵗ Century, we have the privilege of being radical for Christ. Let us revolutionize the world with the word of God.

I am the true vine John 15 1-5
Jesus is the sprouting vine, and God is the Farmer. A Christians life is like a tree branch. It's a line-by-line process you must go through in order to become a fully developed mature Christian. Jesus is the vine that you must be connected to at all times. You will not be productive if you break away from Him. God is the Farmer. He takes away every branch that is not producing any fruit. And every branch that is producing fruit He trims and cleans, so it can be more productive and abundantly flourishing. **Keep growing in Christ!** God will brush you off and He will get rid of everything that does not reflect His Son.

How to study the Bible

Stay attentive and maintain your focus because it is so easy to be distracted by the television, radio, cell phone etc., and if you know that to be true, turn them off.

Study is defined as; the effort to acquire knowledge, as by reading, observation, or research; to give careful thought to; contemplate; to ponder; reflect.

From left to right: My Sister Stephanie Baines, My Niece Brandie White and Myself Yvette Murphy

What a blessing it is when family come together to study as well as have a few laughs.

Always have books, materials, etc., that will make studying easier for you. While studying the King James Version Bible (KJV) have one or more of these bibles at hand to assist you doing your time of studying, for example: Amplified Bible (AMP), New King James Version (NKJV), New International Version (NIV) etc., to help you relate to the King James Version because it can be challenging. Also, when reading, do not forget to write down what book of the bible along with the verse(s) you are studying, it is also good to have a dictionary on hand to define words you may not know and always take notes and put them in a safe place because you will need them again.

During your study time, choose your favorite scripture(s) and memorize it or them. When studying, God will give you a new understanding of scriptures that you have read before. You may have read it a couple of times and when you read it again, you may say I didn't see this before. Or, you might say I have a better understanding of this scripture. Yes, you do because God threw in a couple of nuggets for you to take from it. Keep your eyes and ears open because God will broaden your understanding! Proverbs 4:5-7 (KJV) Get wisdom, get understanding: forget it not; neither decline from the words of my mouth. Forsake her not and she shall preserve thee: love her, and she shall keep thee. Wisdom is the principal thing; therefore, get wisdom: and with all thy getting get understanding.

Let your heart be opened to receive wisdom and understanding. Do not walk away from these words. Solomon is giving you fatherly advice on how to live. You may be saying, What does this have to do with studying the bible? Everything. You are getting information from the Word of God about what happened in the past. The word is speaking about the present day. And the word is speaking about what will occur in the future. In [Ecclesiastes 1:9-10 NLT] says; History merely repeats itself. It has all be done before. Nothing under the sun is truly new. Sometimes people say, "Here is something new. But actually it is old; nothing is ever truly new. It's just a new face repeating what has been done before it's just recycled actions.

Studying helps you to understand what you are facing or have faced is nothing new. There's someone in the Bible who had a similar problem and God delivered them. He is willing and able to free you as well. He freed the children of Israel out of bondage after 40 years. He is freeing people today. No matter what you are facing, God is not working it out, He has already worked it out. God is not caught of guard about no one's situation.

Be encouraged! The Word of God is a study guide for our lives. Now is your time to run towards wisdom. She will be a fence around you. Get understanding. She will make your life delightful. She will adorn your life with grace.

We are enjoying studying God's word.

Feasting on the Word is food for our soul and joy to our hearts.

Worship

Psalm 95:6 (AMPC) Oh come, let us worship and bow down: let us kneel before the Lord our Maker [in reverent praise and supplication].

Psalm 96:9 (AMPC) O worship the Lord in the beauty of holiness; tremble before and reverently fear Him, all the earth.

Worship is your intimate (personal) time with God, and it can be done privately or corporately. Private worship is just you and God. While in private allow Holy Spirit to pray through you to the Father or pray in your own language. You can play music, sing, clap your hands, dance and some people even laugh. In laughing they are not laughing at the people or what is going on, they have a laughing spirit. Corporate worship is similar to private the only difference is other people are worshipping with you. As you are in worship, going into God's presence is totally up to you! How far do you want and are willing to go? If you want to go all the way, you must be willing to allow Holy Spirit entrance and let Him escort your spirit into the Holy of Holies (God's dwelling place). In doing so, you are emphasizing and acknowledging your respect and love to Him. You're expressing your thankfulness and gratitude to Him. You're letting Him know who and what He is in your life and no one can go before God like you can. You are also demonstrating to Him how much you love, honor, revere and appreciate Him as well as for all He's done and is doing in your life.

John 4: 23-24 (KJV) But the hour cometh, and now is, when the true worshippers shall worship the Father in spirit and in truth: for the Father seeketh such to worship him. God is a Spirit: and they that worship him must worship him in spirit and in truth.

Worship is not your prayer of request to God, but this is your one on one (Father, son or daughter) time together. God our Father wants a son or daughter relationship with you and it is an honor for God to want kinship with you. Worship was put in you from the Father, and it is your duty to give it back to Him. Do not abandon the gift(s) He has given you but you need to press the **on** button for it to be activated! He's seeking for the true worshippers. God sees you, so lets not fake it. You should always give God your best and do what He has deposited into your heart to do. There are some things we will have to give up, in order to be pleasing to the Lord. Worship is not a time for you to give Him your issues, problems, needs or wants. But it is your time of adoration to Him. This is about giving the Lord reverence and exalting Him because of His love, faithfulness and grace toward you. You should be in a posture of thanksgiving to the Father and lifting your hands and voice in awe before Him for your life and what He means to you. Thank Him for a memory, that's all it takes for you to think on how God sent his Son into the world not to judge the world, but to save the world through him. [Refer to: John 3:17 NLT] Give Him your genuine worship. **Don't hold back! Go all the way, because it does take all that and MORE!**

Reconciliation

Reconciliation: to reestablish a close relationship, as in a marriage.

II Corinthians 5:19 [AMPC] It was God [personally present] in Christ, reconciling and restoring the world to favor with Himself, not counting up and holding against [men] their trespasses [but cancelling them], and committing to us the message of reconciliation (of the restoration of favor).

God has looked passed the sin of the world and brought us back to Himself. After all, Jesus went to Calvary and voided out our sins forever. At one time man's relationship with God was torn apart but Jesus became the Lamb Who was slain so that we [mankind] would have our relationship restored. God wanted a relationship with us and we needed to be reconnected with Him and not only when life's trouble comes upon us but always! He is our (GPS) and the only One Who knows what's best for us. Hallelujah God!

We were separated from God at one time but because of Jesus, (believers) have the opportunity to be in unity with God; Jesus Christ who knew no sin, mended the relationship between God and man by dying on the cross for our sins. He has qualified us to be the righteousness of God. Thank You Jesus!

For God made Christ, who never sinned, to be the offering for our sin, so that we could be made right with God through Christ. **(2 Corinthians 5:21)**

Listed below are a few scriptures on reconciliation:

But God showed his great love for us in this way, Christ died for us while we were still sinners. And since we have been made right in God's sight by the blood of Christ, he will certainly save us from God's condemnation. For since our friendship with God has been restored by the death of his Son while we were still his enemies, he will certainly save us from God's condemnation. So now we can rejoice with God because our Lord Jesus Christ has made us friends with God. **(Romans 5:8-11)**

Together with one body, Christ reconciled both groups to God by means of his death on the cross, and our hostility toward each other was put to death. **(Ephesians 2:16)**

For the wages of sin is death, but the gift of God is eternal life in Christ Jesus our Lord. **(Romans 6:23)**

We should always be thankful because death brought us back to God. Jesus Christ was obedient until death on the cross. He never complained because He knew what the results was going to be from His obedience. So, as we meditate on all that Christ did for us, let's give Him our best. We would not have made it without Him. He is our Debt Resolving King. Glory in the Highest.

Communion

John 3:16 [KJV] For God so loved the world, that he gave his only begotten Son, that whosoever believeth in him should not perish, but have everlasting life.

Romans 5:8-9 [NIV] But God demonstrates his own love toward us in this: While we were still sinners, Christ died for us. Since we have been justified by his blood, how much more shall we be saved from God's wrath through Him.

I Corinthians 11: 23-32 (KJV)
For I have received of the Lord that which also I delivered unto you, That the Lord Jesus the same night in which he was betrayed took bread: And when he had given thanks, he brake it, and said, Take, eat: this is my body, which is broken for you: this do in remembrance of me. After the same manner also he took the cup, when he had supped saying, This cup is the new testament in my blood: this do ye, as oft as ye drink it, in remembrance of me. For as often as ye eat this bread, and drink this cup, ye do shew the Lord's death till he come. Wherefore whosoever shall eat this bread, and drink this cup of the Lord, unworthily, shall be guilty of the body and blood of the Lord. But let a man examine himself, and so let him eat of that bread, and drink of that cup. For he that eateth and drinketh unworthily, eateth and drinketh damnation to himself, not discerning the Lord's body. For this cause many are weak and sickly among you, and many sleep. For if we would judge ourselves, we should not be judged. But when we are judged, we are chastened of the Lord, that we should not be condemned with the world.

Paul has given us step by step information on how to acknowledge our individual service of the Lord's Supper.

Take a minute to examine yourself. You do not want to eat of the Lord's Supper unworthily.

Here are a few examples that you may ask the Lord to forgive you before you take communion.

You may have had an argument with your husband, wife, children etc.
You are texting while in church.
You did not allow someone to sit next to you, instead you put your....
You were in a yelling match with a driver who cut in front of you.
You were in the grocery store and someone accidentally bumped into you and before they could say excuse me, you got mad.
Your co-worker talked about you and you were told about.

Paul begins with I received of the Lord that which I delivered unto you:
Paul was speaking of Himself and acknowledging that Jesus took the death penalty for our sins according to the Scriptures. He was buried in a tomb of Joseph from the city of Arimathea, a disciple of Jesus but secretly because he was afraid of the Jewish Leaders. [See: John 19:38-42] but three days later He rose from the dead [Refer to: I Corinthians 15:3-5]

That the Lord Jesus on the same night in which He was betrayed:
Jesus instituted the Lord's Supper with His disciples [Mark 14:22-26] and afterwards, He took with Him, Peter, James and John to the Garden of Gethsemane; He needed some alone time with the Father. He was about to face a very difficult time and the purpose of why He came to earth [John 3:16]. He was about to give up His life for the sin of the world. He prayed Father, if it is Your will, take this cup away from Me; nevertheless "not My will, but Yours be done." Then an angel appeared to Him from heaven, strengthening Him. And being in agony... [Luke 22:42-44 NKJV]. After this prayer and visitation from the angel, Jesus went over to the disciples and found them sleep again knowing that their hearts were grieved

because of these words He spoke previously to them. I have desired to eat this Passover with you before I suffer, for I say to you… [See Luke 22:15-16 NKJV]. Now the hour was at hand for Judas to betray Him with a kiss and give Him over to sinners [Mark 14:43-50]. Finally, He said to them let us be going but while He was speaking, Judas and a great multitude approached them with swords and clubs in their hands. These men were the chief priests, the scribes and the elders [religious leaders.] During the time of Jesus' arrest and crucifixion, He would face the utmost rejection from the people, the scribes, His disciples and His brief separation from God.

In remembrance of Me:

Eating of the bread or wafer is symbolic of Jesus' body which was wounded (receiving 39 stripes on his back) for the wrong we did, crushed for the evil we did, the punishment He suffered that brought us reconciliation. (Jesus made it possible for us to return back to God as well as for us to be adopted into the family of God) and by His wounds we are healed [Refer to: Isaiah 53:5].

Drinking of the wine or juice is symbolic of the perfect bloodshed on the cross that made us justified declared righteous which cleanses us from all sin. [See I John 1:7]. Jesus who knew no sin, was found guilty and sentenced to death. But on the third day, He stepped out of the tomb of **"I'm Alive"** and clothed Himself in **"I did it for you."**

Isaiah, one of the major prophets of the Old Testament recorded:

In Isaiah 9:6 [KJV] For unto us a child is born, unto us a son is given: and the government shall be upon his shoulder: and his name shall be called Wonderful, Counsellor, The mighty God, The everlasting Father, The Prince of Peace.

Isaiah 53:5-6 [KJV] But he was wounded for our transgressions, he was bruised for our iniquities: the chastisement of our peace was upon him;

and with his stripes we are healed. All we like sheep have gone astray: and the Lord hath laid on him the iniquity of us all.

In this twenty first century, you will face distractions, but do not let them keep you from accomplishing the plan God has for you. Paul tells us in [Romans 8:35-37 NKJV] Who shall separate us from the love of Christ? Shall tribulation, or distress, or persecution, or famine, or nakedness, or peril or sword? As it is written: For Your sake we are killed all day long; We are accounted as sheep for the slaughter. Yet in all these things we are more than conquerors through Him who loved us.

The time is now (at this very moment) for us to be radical for Christ, especially when we are under pressure. Trust and believe Jesus is our bridge over agitated waters. He is our Safe Place no matter what is trying to derail you, stay your course, the turbulence is coming to an end and your enemies are going down! [Satan and his followers]. Your fight is spiritual and not flesh and blood; and our weapons are not of this world (refer to Ephesians 6:10-18). Everything that you do for Christ, your enemies will try to frustrate and stop you from your God given assignment. **Frustrate your frustration!** Let them see your smile; give it your all because whatever you go or going through has an expiration date and you will overcome every trial in temptation.

A New Way of Thinking

Romans 12:1-2 (KJV)
I beseech you therefore, brethren, by the mercies of God, that ye present your bodies a living sacrifice, holy, acceptable unto God, which is your reasonable service.

And be not conformed to this world: but be ye transformed by the renewing of your mind; that ye may prove what is that good, and acceptable, and perfect will of God.

Romans 12:1-2 (NLT)
And so, dear brothers and sisters, I plead with you to give your bodies to God because of all he has done for you. Let them be a living and holy sacrifice—the kind he will find acceptable. This is truly the way to worship him. Don't copy the behavior and customs of this world, but let God transform you into a new person by changing the way you think. Then you will learn to know God's will for you, which is good and pleasing and perfect.

Paul makes an appeal for us to make a change in our entire lives. We should be willing to undergo a spiritual transformation for God. This would be a life worth living when He is the Director who directs your every step, moment by moment. Let him think for you and allow Him to be your driver. For He knows where you need to go and the time you need to arrive. It would be so much easier for you to go about life without confusing yourself. He has the best answers for all of life's questions. Let the Lord invade every area of your life. You no longer need to recycle those thoughts over and over again. It is time for an upgrade in your life and for you to begin moving into what He has and wants to release to you. The Lord wants complete access so that you can work the works He has assigned for your life. Let the old mindset go so that you can say yes to God.

Here is what needs to be done: **[II Corinthians 10:5 [KJV]** Casting down imaginations, and every high thing that exalteth itself against the knowledge of God, and bringing into captivity every thought to the obedience of Christ.

Be aware of the thoughts you entertain and do not consider any negative one. For they are walls that stands tall and proud against the knowledge of our All Knowing God. Philippians 4:8(NLT) tells us, And now, dear brothers and sisters, one final thing. Fix your thoughts on what is true, and honorable, and right, and pure, and lovely and admirable. Think about things that are excellent and worthy of praise. So, when you change the way you think, you will walk into your purpose.

Be encouraged!

Prayer/How to Pray

Prayer means an offering devout (sincere, earnest and heartfelt) request, praise and thanks to God.

Praying to God is the beginning of a relationship and you should always begin your day with prayer.

Have you ever said to yourself, I don't know how to pray or I need someone to teach me how to pray? Do not be nervous and do not be ashamed.

Jesus was teaching on the Mount to his disciples in Matthew 6:5. He told them not to be like the hypocrites when the pray... And, in Matthew 6:8 Therefore do not be like them...

Matthew 6:9-13 [NKJV]
In this manner, therefore, pray: Our Father in heaven, Hallowed be Your name, Your kingdom come. Your will be done. On earth, as it is in heaven. Give us this day our daily bread. And forgive us our debts, As we forgive our debtors, And do not lead us not into temptation, But deliver us from the evil one. For Yours is the kingdom, and the power and the glory, forever. Amen.

And one of Jesus' disciples said to Him in Luke 11:1-2 "Lord, teach us to pray...So He said to them, "When you pray, say:

Luke 11:2a-4 [NKJV]
Our Father in heaven, Hallowed be Your name. Your kingdom come. Your will be done. On Earth as it is in heaven. Give us day by day our daily bread. And forgive us our sins, For we also forgive everyone who is indebted to us. And do not lead us into temptation, But deliver us from the evil one.

Paul is the Author of Romans, Philippians, I & II Thessalonians:

There are times when you will not have any words, it could be humming, shaking or crying that causes you to be speechless but remember, we have the Spirit Himself to pray on our behalf. Let's not be discouraged but be encouraged because our Helper knows exactly what you're going through and He petitions God in the matter.

Romans 8:26-27 [AMP]
In the same way the Spirit [comes to us and] helps us in our weakness. We do not know what prayer to offer or how to offer it as we should, but the Spirit Himself [knows our need and at the right time] intercedes on our behalf with sighs and groaning to deep for words. And He who searches the hearts knows what the mind of the Spirit is, because the Spirit intercedes [before God] on behalf of God's people in accordance with God's will.

In spite of circumstances beyond your control don't allow that to silence you or keep you from exalting the Lord.

Philippians 4:4-7 [NIV]
Rejoice in the Lord always: I will say it again: Rejoice! Let your gentleness be evident to all. The Lord is near. Do not be anxious about anything, but in every situation, by prayer and petition, with thanksgiving, present you requests to God. And the peace of God, which transcends all understanding, will guard your hearts and your minds in Christ Jesus.

We are to pray everyday and give thanks because the Lord wants us to acknowledge Him. He has been to good to us for us to be silent but to express gratitude for all he has done for us.

I Thessalonians 5:17-18 [KJV]
Pray without ceasing. In every thing give thanks: for this is the will of God in Christ Jesus concerning you.

As a believer "prayer" should be our daily on-going appetite [a desire, zeal, yearning.]

How awesome it is to see the children praying to God just before going to Sunday School at Christians of Burlington County [CBC], Westhampton, NJ.

[Proverbs 22:6 KJV] Train up a child in the he should go: and when he is old, he will not depart from it.

From left to right: Mariella Rogers, Isaiah Rogers, Amaan Ridley, Amare Ridley and Cameron Davis.

The Ultimate Life Exchange

II Corinthians 5:17 [KJV]
Therefore, if any man be in Christ, he is a new creature: old things are passed away; behold, all things are become new.

II Corinthians 5:17 [AMPC]
Therefore if any person is [engrafted] in the (Messiah) he is a new creation (a new creature altogether); the old [previous moral and spiritual condition] has passed away. Behold, the fresh and new has come.

If any man: Paul's statement welcomes any and everyone, know matter what your background may be. Come and be part of the ultimate life change. Let the new you come forward while the old you be laid to rest. The old you has been transformed and Christ in you is on display and now you are to follow in His footsteps. Begin to see the world through the lenses of our Great Transformer Christ Himself. Take joy in knowing that Jesus will do what is needed so that God the Father can get the glory. Humble yourself and be patient in the process.

The new man has been restored and regenerated by Jesus entitling us to be what God said in [Genesis 1:26 NKJV] Let Us make man in Our image, according to Our likeness...It's time to take our rightful position again and be the ruler's God intended for us to be. We are Kingdom Ruler's and Royalty is in our DNA. No longer do we move aside but we get in and step into "Take Back" mode! Take Back..., Take Back..., Take back...!

The old man no longer exists. The old you dealt with the people, places and things. There were people you allowed in your circle that caused you..., there were places you should not have gone, and things that you...!

Jesus has made your life clean and productive. Stay connected to the vine. **John 15:1-3 [NCV]** I am the true vine; my Father is the gardener. He cuts off every branch of mine that does not produce fruit. And he trims and cleans every branch that produces fruit so that it will produce even more fruit. You are already clean because of the words I have spoken to you.

This discipleship book will encourage the hearts of those who are willing to follow Christ and those who has already made the choice above all choices to follow Him. I have found in my walk with Christ to be the best decision and the wisest one ever. I have been following the Lord since January of 1999 wholeheartedly and at that time I was experiencing some health issues. It was life or death for me and through my tears, I was saying to God day and night, no one can heal me but You. On May 18, 1999 at the age of twenty-nine (29) I was diagnosed with Relapsing-Remitting Multiple Sclerosis. This is my challenge but as a Champion I always win. Though I get knocked down, I always jump back into "Bounce Back mode." And I encourage you to bounce back because Champions don't quit. Keep your head up above your shoulders with God being your Defender [Psalm 89:18 KJV.]

Yvette M. Murphy

www.ingramcontent.com/pod-product-compliance
Lightning Source LLC
Chambersburg PA
CBHW031239120626
46545CB00003B/1201